I had warned Ms. Garcia that the school music department was depleted, but she hadn't believed me and had laughed it off.

By the time we got back to the classroom, Ms. Garcia had recovered some of her exuberance. "There appears to be a small hurdle to overcome in my plans to turn you all into musicians," she told the class. "We need to buy some new instruments."

We all looked at each other. Us? Buy new instruments? We told her that our school could hardly afford computers and gym equipment, so we couldn't see the school using its scarce funds to buy musical instruments.

Ms. Garcia just smiled and said, "Then we'll have to raise the money ourselves, won't we?" Her enthusiasm continued, and her voice went up an octave. "Come on, guys. I'd like you to brainstorm some imaginative ideas for raising money, and I'll call the music store at lunchtime today to check out their prices."

Ms. Garcia sure wasn't wasting any time, and ignoring our groans, she told us to get into groups and to start thinking of ways to raise money.

"We could have a bake sale," said Natalie.

"That's imaginative," said Ramiro, and he rolled his eyes. "Anyway, bake sales aren't allowed at school."

I looked at my watch. It was five minutes to twelve, and Dad was picking me up early for a checkup at the dentist's office. "Sorry, have to go," I said.

It was lucky that no one was around when Dad pulled up. Our car was still covered with a blanket of brown dust from our camping trip in the desert.

"The car's really dirty, Dad," I said as I got in. As soon as I said it, I wished I hadn't.

He looked at me sideways. "Thanks, son. I accept your kind offer to clean it."

"I so set myself up for that," I thought as I slumped in the seat. Then as we turned out of the school parking lot, it dawned on me—maybe our group could have a car wash to raise some money.

I turned to Dad. "How much would you pay to have your car cleaned, Dad?"

He pretended to look alarmed, and then he laughed. "I was hoping you'd do it for free."

CHAPTER TWO
The Plan

The next day, when I explained the car wash idea to the rest of my group, they seemed enthusiastic. Tamzin's dad said that we could use the parking lot at his hardware store and he'd supervise us, so then we all raided our homes for buckets and sponges. Natalie's brother, who was an artist, said he'd donate paint and posterboard for signs.

Dad gave me a loan to buy some cleaning products too. "Consider it an investment," he said in the voice he reserved for his clients at the barber shop. "If the enterprise is successful and you prosper, you can pay me back from the profit you make, and if you don't prosper, you can repay me by doing extra chores."

"In that case, I will make extra sure that we prosper," I said, smiling and copying his tone.

Ms. Garcia said she would open a bank account where we could deposit the money we earned, and she also said that she had four free tickets to the new Adventure Extreme park, which she'd give to the group that raised the most money.

Things started to get more competitive after that, and all the kids became secretive about their fundraising schemes. "A piece of cake. We're going to win easily," I heard Jaden Smezek whisper to one of his team.

Jaden is one of those smart kids who has a knack for winning every competition. He was still gloating about winning first place in the science fair when he'd designed a self-filling dog bowl and gotten his picture in the paper.

We planned to hold the car wash three Saturdays in a row, starting the next week, so we had a lot to do. Mom took me to the grocery store to buy the cleaning products, Tamzin roped off a corner of her dad's parking lot, and on Friday after school, everyone came around to my place to work on the signs.

Before we could make the signs, we had to figure out how much to charge. In the end, we decided to offer three different services: a basic clean for $5, a clean and vacuum for $7, and a deluxe clean and polish for $10.

On Saturday, Mom said she'd take me down to the lot on her way to work. As we drove, I was feeling pretty good about everything. The car wash had been my brainchild, we were super-organized, and I had a feeling we were in for a very successful day. "What are you smiling about?" Mom asked.

"Just imagining a day at Adventure Extreme," I said.

My cheerful mood evaporated like water on a hot sidewalk when we pulled up at the lot and I looked across the road. In a lot next to the gas station, a car wash was in full swing, and motorists who'd just filled up were being captured by a squad of kids in T-shirts with "School Fundraiser" printed on their backs. There in the middle of all this activity, Jaden Smezek was washing down the hood of a long, white station wagon, wielding a big yellow sponge and flashing a dazzling smile.

"My car needs washing," said Mom quickly. I knew she was only trying to help, but somehow I felt worse.

Mom must have put out an SOS after she left because soon other family members started arriving. Ramiro's granddad brought his car in for a wash even though it was spotless, and a few minutes later, Tamzin's dad arrived and said his van needed washing.

After the flurry of family vehicles, there was a gap of an hour when not a single car pulled in, and meanwhile across the road, Jaden and his mob could hardly keep up with the demand. I threatened to change our signs to "Car WashOUT."

Later I noticed a blue SUV pull out of the gas station and head our way. It had mud-caked tires and dirty windows and was covered in dust and grime. "This'll be a challenge," I said.

The driver must have read my mind. "As you can see, this car's long overdue for a bath," he said, climbing out. "I'll have the deluxe treatment, please."

We sweated over that vehicle for a quarter of an hour while the man sat on a nearby bench and watched us work. Tamzin and I soaped the outside while Natalie vacuumed the inside and Ramiro used a vinyl cleanser on the dashboard. After we had finished polishing, you could see your reflection in the paintwork.

"Impressive job," said the man, and he glanced across the road. "I see you have some competition."

I twirled my squeegee and shrugged. "Nothing we can't handle," I replied, trying to sound nonchalant.

"That's the spirit," the man laughed. After he left, we realized he'd given us a generous tip.

CHAPTER THREE

Fundraising Flops

Even with the extra money from the man in the SUV, there were only a few lonely bills in our money container. At three o'clock, we decided to call it a day. I noticed Jaden and his crew were also packing up, and when he saw me watching, he made a big deal about lifting their heavy cash box.

~~~~~

"So how did it go?" asked Ms. Garcia on Monday. I knew the most important thing was raising enough money to buy new instruments, but I could hardly bear to look at Jaden, who was bursting to answer. His group had raised $300, but at least we weren't the only ones whose fundraisers were a flop. Another group had started a dog-walking service and lured only two customers, and some other kids had offered to clean windows but had forgotten they'd need a ladder.

"It's still early, and I think you've all done really well," said Ms. Garcia. "This is a fantastic start to our savings fund."

Ms. Garcia told us that she'd opened the bank account and she'd deposit the money from the weekend's ventures so it would start earning interest. When she put each group's total on the chart, Jaden Smezek's team was at the top.

"Maybe we should do something totally different," said Ramiro at lunchtime.

"Like what?" asked Tamzin.

"I don't know, but something more profitable," said Ramiro.

"We don't have time to organize anything else," said Natalie, who looked totally fed up.

I thought for a moment. "Maybe we could just do what we did, but do it better."

"The only way we could do better is to move someplace else so we're not competing with Jaden," said Tamzin.

"It's too late to find another location," said Ramiro.

"Why don't we advertise?" I suggested. "Tell people why our service is better."

Tamzin and Natalie nodded. It was worth a try, so we made posters with "Superior Car Care" written in big, bright letters and with our services and prices listed underneath. Then we posted our advertisements in store windows, on community bulletin boards, and even at the gas station across the road.

As the weekend loomed, we were all feeling pretty nervous. We knew there was a risk the car wash would be a flop again.

Then on Saturday, I woke to the sound of strong winds buffeting the house. "That's all we need!" I thought. Dad dropped me at the lot early because we wanted to get started before Jaden and his team.

"Good luck," he said, honking his horn as he pulled away.

"We'll need it," mumbled Ramiro, the wind spraying around the water he was hosing into two water buckets.

CHAPTER FOUR

A Return Customer

The morning started brilliantly. Three cars came in shortly after we started, but then Jaden and his team got into full swing, and after that, we watched the lines begin across the road.

"This is so embarrassing," groaned Tamzin.

I had to hand it to Jaden. Setting up next to the gas station had been a smart move. There was no shortage of customers, and there was an area where drivers could get out of the wind while they waited.

After lunch, it seemed to get colder, and we were ready to pack up for the day. An icy breeze swept across the lot. We were gathering our gear when the blue SUV from the previous week pulled in.

"Morning, or should I say afternoon?" said the man, looking at his watch. "How's it all going?"

"Awful weather," I said, "and that hasn't helped."

He pulled his collar up against the wind. "I have a proposition for you," he said. The man introduced himself as Mr. Forrest, and he and Tamzin's father shook hands. He explained that he was running a big car fair and had a warehouse full of vehicles that needed cleaning.

"If you guys can do the same job on them as you did on this," he said, leaning against his SUV, "then the job is yours."

We couldn't believe it. "What do you think, Mr. Anton?" I asked Tamzin's dad.

"Sounds like a great idea," he replied.

Mr. Forrest offered us wages of $20 a car, saying we could work over the next two weekends and bring as many helpers as we wanted.

When we told Ms. Garcia on Monday, she was as excited as we were. "We'll be able to earn enough money for our instruments in no time!" she said.

For the next two weekends, our whole class, including Ms. Garcia, washed cars. It was hard work, but it was lots of fun too.

At first, Jaden was grumpy about the change of plans, but when Ms. Garcia said we could all afford to go to Adventure Extreme now, he was as excited as everyone else. And what's more, when Mr. Forrest found out what we were raising money for, he matched our total savings, dollar for dollar. After buying the musical instruments and paying for Adventure Extreme, we had $1,000 left over, so Ms. Garcia put it in another bank account that earned a higher interest rate. "That can go toward the grand piano," I joked to Ramiro.

"There is nothing like the smell of new instruments," sighed Ms. Garcia a few weeks later. She had her nose pressed up against an electric guitar.

Our school principal was amazed that we'd raised the money to buy new instruments, and during an assembly, she invited us all on stage.

"As a result of Room 501's efforts, the school has a collection of wonderful new musical instruments," she boomed across the sea of heads. "They have proven that if you really want something, you can achieve it."

Ms. Garcia was standing next to me. "Within a few months, we'll be playing on that stage," she whispered.

It was hard to imagine because our early lessons sounded like a bunch of hyenas fighting with a herd of noisy elephants, but we had faith in Ms. Garcia. One thing we'd learned was that when she set her mind on something, it usually worked out.

Summarize

Use important details from *Cleaning Up the Competition* to summarize how the students got the musical instruments they needed. Your graphic organizer may help.

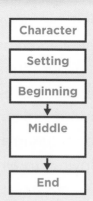

Character

Setting

Beginning
↓
Middle
↓
End

Text Evidence

1. What kind of fiction is this? How can you tell? GENRE

2. In Chapter 1, what events led up to the narrator's coming up with the idea of having a car wash to raise money? SEQUENCE

3. What does *enterprise* mean on page 5? Reread the sentence to help you figure it out. SENTENCE CLUES

4. Write about the events that led up to Mr. Forrest's asking the students to clean his cars.
WRITE ABOUT READING

Compare Texts
Read to find out how banks help people get what they need.

Growing Money

Money may not grow on trees, but one place where it does grow is in the bank. One of the reasons for putting money in the bank, besides keeping it safe, is that it will earn interest. Interest is the money the bank pays you to use your money.

In *Cleaning Up the Competition*, the first thing Ms. Garcia did when money started coming in was to deposit it in the bank. She knew it would be safer there. Having a lot of money lying around is not a good idea.

Making a Profit

Banks are businesses, and businesses need to make a profit. Banks make a profit by borrowing money from some customers and lending it to others. What they charge to lend money is more than what they pay to borrow it. The difference is profit.

17

The other reason Ms. Garcia was so eager to put the money in the bank was so it would earn interest. The more money you put in the bank, and the longer you leave it there, the more interest it earns.

Banks affect our lives in so many ways. They help us save for a college education, or loan us money to buy a home or start a business. On a larger scale, they keep economies healthy by financing and advising large companies so they can grow and prosper.

How Does Interest Work?

Room 501 had $1,000 left over after they had bought the musical instruments. If they left that money in the bank for a year, and the bank paid 5 percent annual interest, it would be worth $1,050 at the end of that year. The $50 is the fee the bank would pay for being able to use the money for a year.

There are different kinds of banks, but the ones most of us deal with are called commercial banks. These are the banks that hold our accounts and lend us money to buy things like homes and cars. Commercial banks usually have lots of branches, and chances are, there is one close to where you live.

Room 501's Musical Instrument Fund

- Initial deposit
- Interest earned

(x-axis: JAN – MAR, APR – JUN, JUL – SEP, OCT – DEC)
(y-axis: $0, $250, $500, $750, $1,000, $1,250)

Darren Greenwood/Design Pics

Since modern banks came into existence, they have been in a constant state of change. One of the fastest growing areas is the development of online, or Internet, banking. Instead of going to a bank to make a transaction, people can make deposits and withdrawals, pay bills, and move money around with the click of a mouse.

Online banking is only one of the many ways that banking has changed. People carry less cash today, using a bank card instead, and if they do need cash, they use automatic teller machines (ATMs). Despite advances in technology, the main function of a bank is still to provide a secure place to keep money.

Make Connections

How do banks help people get what they need?
ESSENTIAL QUESTION

What did you learn from *Cleaning Up the Competition* and *Growing Money* about the ways banks help people? **TEXT TO TEXT**

Focus on
Literary Elements

Similes Similes are figures of speech that compare two things by using the words *like* or *as*. For example, *busy as a bee* means very busy.

Read and Find On page 7 in *Cleaning Up the Competition*, Jake's "cheerful mood evaporated like water on a hot sidewalk." This means his mood quickly changed and he became grumpy.

Your Turn

With a partner, look around the classroom. Pick something to describe using a simile. After you've thought of a few together, think of one on your own. Write down your similes and share them with another group.